IMAGES
of America

MOBILE
AND THE
EASTERN SHORE

MOBILE AND THE EASTERN SHORE

Frye, Nancy, and Tracy Gaillard

First published 1997
Copyright © Frye, Nancy, and Tracy Gaillard, 1997

ISBN 0-7524-0546-2

Published by Arcadia Publishing,
an imprint of the Chalford Publishing Corporation,
One Washington Center, Dover, New Hampshire 03820.
Printed in Great Britain

Library of Congress Cataloging-in-Publication Data applied for

This book is dedicated to Helen Amante Gaillard,

and to the memories of Mabel Toulmin and Nedra Greer.

Contents

Introduction		7
1.	Pieces of History	9
2.	Life and Commerce	27
3.	Places to See	49
4.	People	65
5.	Playgrounds to the Hall of Fame	85
6.	The Eastern Shore	99
7.	Changes	119
Acknowledgments		128

One of Mobile's founders, Pierre Le Moyne, Sieur d'Iberville, was a French-Canadian naval hero who led an expedition to the Gulf Coast in 1699. He first built a fort near the current site of Ocean Springs, Mississippi, then moved the garrison in 1702 to the original site of Mobile—a bluff on the river north of Mobile Bay. His younger brother, Jean Baptiste Le Moyne, Sieur de Bienville, supervised construction of the Mobile fort, along with a rough collection of huts. D'Iberville died in 1706, the victim of a fever, leaving Bienville to oversee the colony. (Historic Mobile Preservation Society.)

Introduction

The Spanish explorers were the first to see it. They came from the south on a mission of greed, sailing into the Gulf and then to the shallows of Mobile Bay. In 1519, the procession began with Alonso Pineda, who was followed by Narvaez and DeSoto, all of them seeking precious metal from the earth. They didn't find very much in the Alabama forests, and Mobile was an afterthought in their diaries. But then in 1558, another Spaniard, Guido de las Bazares, sailed into the bay and immediately recommended to King Phillip II that the Spanish build a permanent village on its shores.

The first to attempt to build such a village was by Tristan de Luna, a conquistador who came north from Vera Cruz, only to be greeted by a hurricane that struck the bay at the moment of his arrival. His supplies were lost, and in the spring of 1561, less than two years into his mission, his colonists were forced to return to Mexico.

But success soon followed from a different direction—from the French explorers moving south out of Canada. In 1699, Pierre Le Moyne, Sieur d'Iberville led an expedition to Mobile Bay, and three years later, he established a fort on the Mobile River. In 1711, the garrison was moved to the present site of Mobile, and the area soon became a fur-trading port—a frontier settlement with a brick-walled fort and rough wooden huts. Its population grew slowly in the eighteenth century, surviving yellow fever and wars with the Indians and then, in 1763, a transfer of political control to the British.

For the next fifty years, Mobile was caught in a swirl of international competition, as British rule gave way to the Spanish, and then to the Americans in 1813. Soon, however, the fur-trading village now just over a hundred years old would become something more—a rich and graceful antebellum city where fortunes were made in the export of cotton and great white mansions took their place among the oaks. By the 1830s, there were abundant churches, theaters, and a college, and the city developed a new personality—an antebellum charm that has yet to disappear.

Many a visitor has remarked on its beauty, from the Marquis de Lafayette in 1825, to Woodrow Wilson and Jack Kerouac, and Mobilians are proud of that part of their history—a refinement toughened by their frontier past. But there has always been another side to the story, a harsher reality hidden by the grace. Among other things, beginning with the institution of slavery, the city has been faced with the issue of race. The results have been mixed. Although slavery flourished in the antebellum South, Mobile was a haven for free blacks as well, and from Reconstruction times to the present, strong black leaders such as John LeFlore have stood firmly for the rights of their own people—and for the larger cause of racial understanding.

There were also whites who were part of that struggle, but Mobile could be cruel. At the turn of the century, its leading newspaper, *The Mobile Register*, championed the cause of disenfranchisement and the systematic imposition of the codes of segregation. In 1904, a black newspaper editor and Republican loyalist, Andrew N. Johnson, was thrown out bodily from Bienville Square, a public park in the heart of downtown, by a mob of whites that included officials from his own party. It was a pivotal moment for Mobile's blacks, a reminder that harsher times were ahead.

Some of them managed to prosper anyway—as athletes, missionaries, musicians, educators—and perhaps they took some ironic comfort in the difficulties afflicting other parts of society. From the Civil War on, Mobile's economy was often in trouble. First came the fall of the cotton market in the years of Reconstruction, a time when Birmingham replaced Mobile as the largest and most promising city in the state. There was a recovery for a while in the twentieth century, driven most powerfully by the engines of war, but there were alternating periods of recession and depression, and in the 1960s, Mobile lost a major Air Force base that had become a cornerstone of the economy.

And yet, through it all, Mobile has survived, still full of pride in its beauty and its past, and it appears to have entered, in the 1990s, another era of promise. Its once-declining downtown area, residential and commercial, has experienced a renaissance in recent years, and for many of the people who are leading that recovery, the key to the future is a healthy appreciation of the past. There are bumper stickers scattered through the city, pushing the cause of historic preservation— "the ultimate recycling," one of them says—and this book is intended as a gesture of support.

We have combed through the rich archives of the city for the images that capture some of Mobile's spirit, and we have sought to put a human face on the story. Our basic understanding comes down to this: It is not necessary to idealize history, to make it unreal, in order to appreciate where we have been. Mobile, like any community, has had its share of struggles through the years, but the thing that sets it apart is its grace, an identity forged from noble aspirations and from the natural and manmade beauty of the place. Those are the things worth keeping alive. We hope this book will contribute to the cause.

Frye Gaillard
Nancy Gaillard
Tracy Gaillard

One
Pieces of History

This square in the heart of downtown Mobile pays tribute to Bienville, one of two French-Canadian brothers given credit in history for the founding of the city. Bienville's role was perhaps most central. In addition to building the original garrison, he made the decision in 1711 to move the village to its current location. Bienville served as governor of French Louisiana, and in the early years Mobile was its capital. It began its life as an earthen fort with thatched-roof huts, but in the 1720s, the fort was strengthened, its exterior bricked for greater protection. By then, however, Bienville had moved the capital of Louisiana, first to Biloxi and then to New Orleans, leaving Mobile to emerge as a rough and hard-scrabble fur-trading community. (Historic Mobile Preservation Society.)

Henri de Tonti was one of the most flamboyant of Mobile's early leaders. A fearless explorer, he had traveled the Mississippi River with LaSalle, floating its length in 1682 and claiming the Mississippi Valley for France. In 1702, de Tonti moved to the Gulf, joining Bienville and d'Iberville in building French forts and helping to establish trading and diplomatic ties with the Indians. The natives admired de Tonti for his courage, and they were fascinated by the iron hook that he wore in place of a hand, which had been mutilated by a grenade. The victim of Mobile's first yellow fever epidemic, de Tonti died in 1704. With his passing, the fledgling town lost its greatest military leader, but managed to survive and slowly grew stronger in its new world environment. (Museum of the City of Mobile.)

A fading sign and a grove of oaks are the modest reminders of a French outpost on Dauphin Island at the mouth of Mobile Bay. Ships with cargoes bound for the fledgling city of Mobile often docked at the island, where the water was deeper. A memorial square on Dauphin Island is named for Antoine de la Mothe Cadillac, the founder of Detroit, later appointed governor of Louisiana. Cadillac didn't care for the assignment, reportedly declaring in one letter home: "This whole continent is not worth having." (W.F. Gaillard.)

One of the peaceful spots in downtown Mobile, the Spanish Plaza was built in tribute to the city's long association with Spain. Spanish explorers first visited the area in the sixteenth century—Alonzo de Pineda in 1519, Panfilo de Narvaez in 1528, and Hernando deSoto around 1540. In addition, the Spanish ruled Mobile from 1780 until the War of 1812. (W.F. Gaillard)

On August 30, 1813, an army of Creek Indians under the leadership of William Weatherford attacked Fort Mims, a flimsy stockade just north of Mobile. They managed to kill most of the people inside—men, women and children—setting off a bloody war that broke the power of the Creek Nation and paved the way for white settlement of Alabama. The Fort Mims massacre, as it became known, was a monument not only to the rage of the Creeks, who resented the gradual white encroachment on their lands, but also to the incompetence of the military commander at the fort. Major Daniel Beasley was so scornful of rumors of an Indian attack that he refused even to shut the stockade gates. In retaliation for the massacre, Gen. Andrew Jackson, pictured above, marched south from Tennessee and defeated the Creeks at the Battle of Horseshoe Bend. From there, Jackson pushed on to Mobile and helped build its defenses against an attack by the British near the end of the War of 1812. (Historic Mobile Preservation Society.)

Barton Academy, one of Mobile's most handsome buildings, was the cornerstone of the first public school system in Alabama. Built in 1836 and designed by the famous architect Thomas James, it became a public school in 1852. Soon after that, the state passed legislation for a public system based on the Mobile model. Today, Barton Academy serves as the central headquarters for the Mobile schools. (W.F. Gaillard.)

The Medical College of Alabama opened its doors in 1859 in Mobile. Its founder, Dr. Josiah Nott, a nationally known physician from South Carolina, traveled extensively in the United States and Europe in order to furnish the school with the most modern technology. In 1894, a group of Birmingham doctors established a rival medical school in their city, and the two groups launched a battle for money in the state legislature. In 1920, Birmingham won, as the lawmakers ended their appropriations to Mobile. (Historic Mobile Preservation Society.)

Ship captain Timothy Maeher, who would become a daring Confederate blockade runner during the Civil War, made his first and most dubious mark on history by bringing the last shipment of African slaves to the United States—more than fifty years after such trade was illegal. There were 116 survivors of the transatlantic voyage, which ended in the port of Mobile in 1859. (Alabama Department of Archives and History.)

This historical marker designates the spot where slaves were sold in downtown Mobile. Ironically, the city was also a haven for free Negroes, dating back to its French and Spanish days. Runaways from deep South plantations would sometimes head for Mobile instead of trying to make the longer journey across the Mason-Dixon line to the North. (W.F. Gaillard.)

Cudjo Lewis, one of the great black leaders in Mobile history, was kidnapped from his native Africa and brought to America on Timothy Maeher's slave ship, *Clotilde*. Freed only a few years later after the War Between the States, he and other Africans who survived that voyage built a community at Magazine Point, north of Mobile, a village they simply called Africa Town. Lewis was an effective spokesman for the Africans and a driving force in the Baptist church that emerged as a center of community life. Until his death in the 1930s, he never lost his desire to go home to his native Africa, where, he said, there were "no white mans." (Erik Overbey Collection, University of South Alabama Archives.)

During the Civil War, the world's first submarine was built in Mobile. Named the *Hunley*, it represented the third attempt by its inventors to construct a boat that would function under water. The curious craft was made out of wood and propelled by a crew turning cranks attached to a propeller. The boat sank twice in the Charleston harbor before it ever saw any combat. On February 17, 1864, shortly after dusk, the *Hunley* once again set out from the harbor and sank the Union warship *Housatonic*. The submarine, however, was blown apart by its own torpedo. Only five sailors died on the *Housatonic*. Among the crew of the *Hunley*, there were no survivors. Later that year, the South suffered a much more devastating blow (see below), losing the battle of Mobile Bay. This sketch of the battle appeared in *Harper's Weekly*, September 10, 1864. (*Official Records of the Union and Confederate Navies of the War of the Rebellion*, Series I, Vol. 15 and *Harper's Weekly*, September 10, 1864, University of South Alabama Archives.)

In 1864, Admiral David Farragut, frumpy and slouched, was an unimposing figure as he commanded the Union assault on Mobile Bay. But his courage was clear as he issued his command: "Damn the torpedoes, full speed ahead!" With the success of his attack, the South lost one of its last remaining seaports, and three months before the presidential election, Abraham Lincoln was presented with a major psychological victory. He won reelection with a mandate to see the war to its finish. (Alexander Foxhall Parker, *The Battle of Mobile Bay*, Boston: A. Williams, 1878; University of South Alabama Archives.)

During the Civil War, Fort Gaines, on the tip of Dauphin Island, guarded the western shore of the Bay, while Fort Morgan guarded the east. With a row of mines stretched between the forts, the defense was thought to be impenetrable. But the mines were corroded from their long exposure to the salt, and when the Union Navy began its assault, most of them simply failed to explode. (S. Blake McNeely Collection, University of South Alabama Archives.)

Fort Morgan, sentinel on the eastern shore of the bay, was reduced almost to rubble during Admiral Farragut's attack. Long since restored, it now stands as a menacing reminder of one of the most critical battles of the war. (Library of Congress, University of South Alabama Archives.)

Confederate Capt. J.W. Whiting was one of the defenders of Fort Morgan during the Battle of Mobile Bay. Twenty-two years later, his commanding officer, R.L. Page, wrote him a letter of recommendation (see below), citing his "gallantry and meritorious conduct." (Erik Overbey Collection, University of South Alabama Archives.)

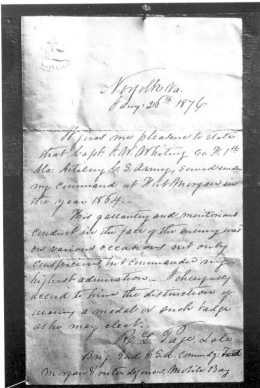

To win the "highest admiration" of Brigadier General R.L. Page was no small accomplishment. Page, the fiery first cousin of Robert E. Lee, had spent most of his life in the navies of the United States and the Confederacy before transferring to the Army to take command of Fort Morgan. Known to his troops as "Old Ramrod," he rejected the surrender offer of the Union commander, David Farragut, even though he knew his position was doomed. "I am prepared to sacrifice life," he wrote, "and will surrender only when I have no means of defense . . ." Two weeks later, on August 22, 1864, that moment came. Even then, Page refused to give up his sword, throwing it away before the formal surrender ceremony. (Erik Overbey Collection, University of South Alabama Archives.)

In 1865, Confederate surgeon Samuel Septimus Gaillard was one of those taken prisoner at the Battle of Fort Blakeley, just north of Mobile. The irony of it was, this last and futile defense of the city came after Robert E. Lee's surrender at Appomattox. (Gaillard family collection.)

In 1898, the battleship *Maine* steamed into Havana harbor, where this photograph was taken. Even before the ship was sunk—an event that triggered the Spanish-American War—Mobile businessmen had petitioned the administration of President McKinley to intervene in Cuba and drive out the Spanish. They argued that American control of Cuba would be good for business, "restoring to us a most valuable commercial field." McKinley eventually followed their advice, and in the words of historians Michael Thomason and Melton McLaurin, "With the outbreak of war, Mobile, and most of America, rejoiced." (Courtesy of the Museum of the City of Mobile and the University of South Alabama Archives.)

With the declaration of war against Spain, H.W. Parlee (pictured here) was one of those who was ready to serve. In those days of rigid racial segregation, Mobile organized two white regiments and a battalion of blacks, the Gilmer Rifles, whose commander, Major Reuben Mims, was ordered to be replaced by a white man. His troops at first refused to accept the leadership of Capt. Robert Lee Bullard, but Bullard soon built a disciplined battalion and defended his men against the harassment they endured in Mobile. The black troops saw no action in Cuba, but later in Anniston, Alabama, several of them were fired on by a group of white soldiers. The blacks fired back, wounding several whites, in what became known, ironically, as the Battle of Anniston. (Erik Overbey Collection, University of South Alabama Archives.)

Fort Morgan, which took a terrible pounding during the Civil War, was restored as a military barracks and artillery base, and it played a role in the Spanish-American War, World War I, and World War II. Today, it stands as a historical treasure on the southwestern tip of Baldwin County, a popular stopping place for tourists. (Fort Morgan Collection, University of South Alabama Archives.)

In April 1917, following the entry of America into World War I, patriotic celebrations in Mobile were common. The one above took place at the railroad station, as soldiers prepared to leave for the war. Mobile mustered more than 17,000 troops, and the city's economy was bolstered by a surge in shipbuilding and trade. (Alabama Department of Archives and History.)

With the bombing of Pearl Harbor on December 7, 1941, Mobilians once again passionately embraced the cause of war. The display above, a flag-raising at the Bemis Brothers Bag Company, was typical of the patriotic mood of the city. Mobile changed dramatically during the war. By 1943, the shipbuilding industry alone employed over 40,000 workers—more than double the total workforce of the city only three years earlier. (Erik Overbey Collection, University of South Alabama Archives.)

When the war effort demanded the services of many Americans, men were not alone in answering the call. More than 350,000 women enlisted in the armed forces during World War II, performing duties ranging from secretarial work to the management of highly classified navigational systems. The four Mobile women pictured here served in the SPARS, an acronym derived from the Coast Guard's motto, Semper Paratus, meaning "always ready." (S. Blake McNeely Collection, University of South Alabama Archives.)

Brookley Field, constructed on the shores of Mobile Bay, transformed what was once a popular recreation area into a war production zone. During World War II, Brookley served as a center for airplane modification and as a major depot for military equipment. Continuing to prosper during the Cold War, it provided jobs to thousands who moved to Mobile, drawn by the promise of wartime employment. (Mobile Municipal Archives.)

Ever since its founding in 1702, Mobile has waged its battle with the elements. Bienville Square, in the heart of downtown, is shown here after a major hurricane in 1906. Like other coastal cities, Mobile simply dug out from the rubble and held its breath each fall as the hurricane season rolled around again. (William E. Wilson Collection, Historic Mobile Preservation Society.)

In 1979, all the communities along Mobile Bay were hammered once again—this time by Hurricane Frederick. This aerial view shows the wreckage not far from Gulf Shores, where all that remained of a row of beach houses were the twisted posts protruding from the ground. (University of South Alabama Archives.)

Bracing themselves against the January cold, these Mobile citizens dedicate a bicentennial marker, commemorating the founding of the city. The marker, erected in 1902, stands at the site of the original French fort on a wooded bluff along the Mobile River, some 55 miles from the mouth of the Bay. In 1711, the settlement was moved to the present site of Mobile. (Historic Mobile Preservation Society.)

History is preserved with a touch of class at the Museum of the City of Mobile, which contains an impressive variety of information both for visitors and residents of the city. Artifacts, portraits, photographs, and displays illustrate Mobile's rich history, with exhibits on subjects ranging from Mardi Gras to slavery. The museum, now located in a former funeral home on Government Street, is scheduled to move before the turn of the century to larger headquarters. (W.F. Gaillard.)

Two
Life and Commerce

Bienville Square, this restful spot in the heart of Mobile, has long been a place of momentary reprieve from the bustling center of the city's commerce. In the area just around it, merchants and shopkeepers have peddled their wares since antebellum times, when Mobile grew into the largest and most prosperous city in the state. The Civil War, however, brought a change. The post-war decline of cotton exports left the city reeling, its population now second to Birmingham's, but by the early years of the twentieth century, Mobile showed signs of economic recovery. More than thirty lumber mills were humming in the area, a deeper ship's channel revitalized the port, and better rail connections to Birmingham and cities to the north raised new optimism about the future. (Historic Mobile Preservation Society.)

On September 8, 1866, Mobile made the cover of *Harper's Weekly*, one of the most popular magazines in the country. This sketch by Special Artist A.R. Ward depicts the teeming commerce of Old Shell Road, which remains, more than 130 years later, one of the major east-west arteries in the city. The canopy of Spanish Moss and live oak limbs has also survived, preserving an aura of Southern grace that has long been one of Mobile's trademarks. (Gaillard family collection.)

At the turn of the century in Mobile County, Bay Shell Road cut a gleaming path through the live oak trees, skirting the western shore of Mobile Bay. In the picture above, a horse and buggy makes its lonely way down the road, which was paved with oyster shells from the Bay. Below, one of the first automobiles in the county shares the same road, foreshadowing the horse and buggy's demise. (William E. Wilson Collection, Historic Mobile Preservation Society.)

Through the years, many of the people in Mobile County have made their living from the water. Here, two fishermen from Bayou La Batre cast their nets in the early morning calm. The village, later made famous in the movie *Forrest Gump*, was established around the property of the first French settler, Joseph Bosarge, who came to the area in 1786. (William E. Wilson Collection, Historic Mobile Preservation Society.)

In addition to providing a living for commercial fishermen, the moss-draped shores of Mobile Bay have been a place of recreation as well. On the western shore, the communities of Bayou La Batre and Coden were a mecca for tourists at the turn of the century, until a series of hurricanes, beginning in 1906, sent the area into a state of decline. Even now, however, the beauty of the bay is a focal point of Mobile's culture. (William E. Wilson Collection, Historic Mobile Preservation Society.)

On a May afternoon in 1909, the regulars gathered at the Coden grocery, lounging on the steps, swapping their stories, while the chickens pecked at the ground out front. Much of Mobile County still bears a resemblance to the farming days of ninety years ago, when life seemed to move at a slower pace. Below, a farmer sits on his fence, while his dog stands guard on the road nearby, and the breeze rustles gently in the live oak trees. (William E. Wilson Collection, Historic Mobile Preservation Society.)

In the summer of 1905, shortly after the automobile appeared in Mobile, a group of orphans gathered on St. Francis Street for their first ride. Photographer William Wilson was there to capture the moment. (William E. Wilson Collection, Historic Mobile Preservation Society.)

The Gould Motor Car Company was one of Mobile's oldest dealerships, specializing in Cadillacs. In 1908, about the time this picture was made, the companies manufacturing Cadillacs, Buicks, and Oldsmobiles began to merge, creating General Motors. (William E. Wilson Collection, Historic Mobile Preservation Society.)

In the early afternoon, pedestrians pause on the southwest corner of Dauphin and Royal Streets beneath the clock at the Zadek Jewelry Company. This busy spot, served by Mobile's trolley system, was also the site of the Hotel Royal. Sadly, the beautiful building with its ornate spires has been replaced. The corner is now the home of the Compass Bank. (William E. Wilson Collection, Historic Mobile Reservation Society.)

Icicles, formed from the water used in fighting a fire, hang from the cast-iron balconies of the Battle House Hotel, long considered one of Mobile's finest. From the time it opened in 1852, the hotel drew rave reviews from its guests, and it was soon restored after this turn-of-the-century blaze. One of the companies doing business in the building, Gulf City Pressing, hung out a sign to reassure its customers that the pace of commerce would not be slowed. (William E. Wilson Collection, Historic Mobile Preservation Society.)

Following Alabama's admission into the Union in 1819, more and more settlers poured into the state, and many of them began to plant cotton, which was exported in the fall and winter through the port of Mobile (see below). The population grew in the 1820s, and the pattern continued until the Civil War, when the cotton trade peaked. By the early years of the twentieth century, the cotton bales being loaded here (left) were no longer the centerpiece of the economy, as lumber from the forests of southern Alabama (pictured above) was being exported at the rate of a billion board-feet a year. (William E. Wilson Collection, Historic Mobile Preservation Society.)

From the vantage point of the 1990s, the bargains are impressive at these two cafes in downtown Mobile, which opened sometime around the turn of the century. The city has long been known for its food—the old-fashioned cooking of places such as these and the seafood restaurants that line the seashore. Gumbo has long been a specialty, along with a Gulf Coast delicacy, fried crab claws, which are seldom found outside of Alabama. (William E. Wilson Collection, Historic Mobile Preservation Society.)

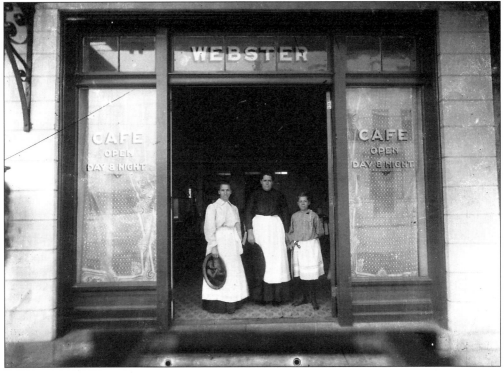

Gordon Smith, bottom row on the far left, was typical of a new generation of merchants who became a mainstay of the Mobile economy. He came to the city in 1899 with 50¢ in his pocket, went to work for a bakery, and in less than a year had saved enough money to start his own. His new plant burned in 1902, but Smith rebuilt it and his bakery today is one of the most recognized names in Mobile business. If the city's economy was built around its port and later a military base by the bay, its merchants also played a vital role. (William E. Wilson Collection, Historic Mobile Preservation Society.)

In the years near the end of the nineteenth century, segregation laws were becoming commonplace in the South, and separation of the races would soon become the social order of the day. In the early 1900s, however, the practice was not yet fully established—and not observed at all in this barber shop in downtown Mobile, where blacks and whites clipped hair at adjoining chairs. (William E. Wilson Collection, Historic Mobile Preservation Society.)

The photographs above and below clearly indicate the pride of Mobile shopkeepers. The R.O. Harris Grocery, pictured here on Dauphin Street, offers a study of how the owner attracted his customers—by aesthetically displaying a variety of fresh fruits and vegetables and carefully arranging the canned goods inside. (William E. Wilson Collection, Historic Mobile Preservation Society.)

Shortly after the turn of the century, these newsboys from the *Mobile Register* posed together on a Mobile street, their supervisors seated in the front. Alabama's first newspapers cropped up in Mobile with the appearance of the *Mobile Sentinel* in 1811 and the *Mobile Gazette* in 1812. Mergers eventually led to the *Mobile Register*, which is still in operation today and has quietly emerged in the 1990s as one of the best newspapers in the South. (Historic Mobile Preservation Society.)

Mule-drawn trolleys were a centerpiece of Mobile transportation throughout much of the nineteenth century, and occasionally, they resulted in curious controversies. In 1871, Lorenzo Wilson, husband of Mobile author Augusta Evans Wilson, was accused by a neighbor of using the mules from a trolley line to plow his own fields. In the family feud that followed, his son Louis Wilson was shot to death by Braxton Bragg, the son of a prominent Mobile judge. No charges were filed, but the city grieved over a senseless killing that didn't have to be. (University of South Alabama Archives.)

Mobile dockworkers and merchant seamen had to be a rough and hardy lot. Their work, most days, was backbreaking at its best, as they moved their cargos from ship to shore, and vice-versa. About the time that lumber replaced cotton as the city's biggest export, bananas emerged as the leading import (see below.) The banana boats of the United Fruit Company made their regular stops at the port, and bananas by the millions were transferred to refrigerated cars and shipped by rail to markets in the North. (Historic Mobile Preservation Society.)

Smoke from another freighter creates a cloud over the *Lord Ormande* as it makes its way into Mobile harbor, escorted by a tug. In the foreground, a stevedore awaits the ship's arrival at the dock. In the 1880s, a major goal of Mobile's commercial establishment was to dredge a deeper channel leading to the port, making it possible for the larger, ocean-going vessels to dock. By the turn of the century, the channel had reached a depth of 27 feet, leaving Mobile competitive with other ports in the South. (Historic Mobile Preservation Society.)

Brookley Field, a U.S. Air Force based named for test pilot Wendell Brookley, who was killed in 1934, served for nearly thirty years as one of the cornerstones of Mobile's economy. At its peak in the early 1960s, it employed more than 15,000 people—nearly 14,000 of them civilians. When the base was closed in 1969, after a flag-lowering ceremony on June 30, the loss of jobs was a devastating blow both to the individuals laid off and to the economic structure of the city. (Mobile Municipal Archives.)

Construction of the University of South Alabama, shown here in an aerial photograph from 1964, began shortly before the closing of Brookley Field. Over the next thirty years, the university emerged as one of Alabama's major centers of learning and one of the major employers in the Mobile area. Gradually, it represented a recovery from the crushing loss of jobs at Brookley Field. (University of South Alabama Archives.)

This Catholic priest, caught in a solemn moment of worship, is part of Mobile's oldest religious tradition. The first Protestant congregation was not organized until 1826, more than 120 years after the founding of the city. The balance, however, shifted quickly after that. By 1860, there were some thirty congregations meeting regularly in Mobile—at least twenty-four of which were Protestant. (Erik Overbey Collection, University of South Alabama Archives.)

Spring Hill College, which opened its doors in 1830, a year after LaGrange, a Methodist institution in northern Alabama, became only the second college in the state. It was part of the legacy of Michael Portier, the first Catholic bishop of Mobile, who was appointed in 1823. Portier's prominence and strong leadership helped establish the city as a place of religious diversity and tolerance. (Erik Overbey Collection, University of South Alabama Archives.)

This Jewish temple, once a handsome presence on Government Street, no longer stands, but the Jewish presence in Mobile is strong. As early as 1763, a New Orleans firm of Jewish merchants headed by Samuel Israel and Alexander Solomons bought property in Mobile and began doing extensive business in the city. The first temple was established in 1844, and in 1853 a Jewish attorney, Philip Phillips, was elected to represent Mobile in Congress. (Historic Mobile Preservation Society.)

Shortly after the turn of the century, a group of black ministers from the Mobile area posed for the camera of William E. Wilson. Their bearing suggests a pride in their calling, but nearly a hundred years later their names are unknown. Though Wilson almost certainly recorded their identities, those records have not survived in the archives. (William E. Wilson Collection, Historic Mobile Preservation Society.)

It's baptism day for the new converts to this African-American congregation in Mobile. The dignity and passion of this sacred occasion were captured by the camera of William E. Wilson. (William E. Wilson Collection, Historic Mobile Preservation Society.)

With glittering lights and elaborate floats, Mardi Gras parades have dominated Mobile's winter season since the years just after the Civil War. Before that time, most of the city's parades and celebrations had taken place on New Year's Eve. But in 1867, the Order Of Myths organized their first Mardi Gras parade, followed by the Infant Mystics in 1869 and the Knights of Revelry in 1870. Historians Melton McLaurin and Michael Thomason argue that the new celebrations helped revive the spirit of the city following the Confederate surrender of 1865. (William E. Wilson Collection, Historic Mobile Preservation Society, below; S. Blake McNeely Collection, University of South Alabama Archives, above.)

While Mobile's wealthy attend the coronations of Mardi Gras royalty, citizens from every walk of life—crowds that measure in the tens of thousands—flock to the Mardi Gras parades. To visitors, it is often an astonishing sight as men, women, and children scramble for the candy, glass beads, and assorted other trinkets—most of them worthless—raining down from the floats. (University of South Alabama Archives.)

The idea of Mardi Gras royalty is taken seriously in Mobile. Here, a recent king and queen, Sumner Adams and Lee Rutherford, are dancing together at their coronation ball. Later, they were married. A generation earlier, the queen's mother, Laura Peebles Rutherford, was also queen . . . and also married her king. (Courtesy of Ann Adams and The Mobile Press Register, Inc.)

In Mardi Gras season, even little girls aspire to royalty. Here, Helen Waggoner poses in her gown and train with a bouquet of roses. Her picture was recently discovered in a basement, buried away in family memorabilia. Exactly when it was taken and how long it had been there, nobody knows. (Courtesy of Ann Adams.)

The Country Club of Mobile is another of the city's oldest social institutions. This original building no longer stands, but in 1997 the club celebrated its centennial birthday. (University of South Alabama Archives.)

The Athelston Club, founded in 1873, was a sanctuary and gathering place for many of Mobile's most prominent businessmen and professional leaders. Many a business deal was struck, and political issues were sometimes discussed, but the club was known also for its elegant balls and programs for the public, including concerts in Bienville Square. (Historic Mobile Preservation Society.)

Three
Places to See

In 1917, Walter and Bessie Bellingrath, the first bottlers of Coca-Cola in Mobile, bought the Bellecamp Lodge on Fowl River just south of Mobile. For the next eighteen years, they worked to transform the rustic lodge into Bellingrath Gardens, one of the most beautiful places in the South. Visitors come year-round from all over the world to see the gardens, which are always in bloom on 65 acres carved from a rain forest. If the Bellingrath's monument to beauty and grace is the scenic highlight of the Mobile area, there are many other attractions that are rich in history and that add their share to the city's reputation. (Erik Overbey Collection, University of South Alabama Archives.)

Memorial Park on Government Street was built in tribute to the Mobile soldiers who died in World War I. The names recorded on the tablets here include some of the most prominent in Mobile's history—Thames, Hamilton, Harris, and Metzger. The memorial itself has been an oasis from the bustle and the swirl of nearby commerce. (W.F. Gaillard.)

Battleship Park, located on the causeway across Mobile Bay, is home to the USS *Alabama*, along with World War II submarines, airplanes, tanks, and other military equipment. The *Alabama* was brought to Mobile in 1965 after school children and businessmen worked together to raise money for the park. (University of South Alabama Archives.)

This reconstruction of Ft. Conde, the first French garrison on the current site of Mobile, stands today against the city's modern skyline. It's a startling change from what the original scene must have been—an earthen fort surrounded by wooden huts. But from those rustic days as a fur-trading post, Mobile began its long and sometimes bumpy evolution into a thriving port and a center of commerce. (W.F. Gaillard.)

The beautiful Conde-Charlotte Museum House is one of Mobile's most historic homes. Located next to the restored Fort Conde, the house, a popular tourist attraction, is now owned and operated by the Colonial Dames of Alabama. Many believe that the house was built on the site of the city's first jail and contains some of the bricks from that original structure. Each room in the house is decorated in the style of a different period, representing the flags under which Mobile was ruled. (W.F. Gaillard.)

The Oakleigh mansion, now operated as a museum by the Historic Mobile Preservation Society, was built in 1833 by Mobile merchant James Roper. The T-shaped structure is nestled on a 3 1/2-acre lot, flanked by towering live oak trees. Inside, the rooms are furnished in authentic antebellum style and are available for visits and tours year-round. (W.F. Gaillard.)

Throughout the city, from simplest home to the finest mansion, many Mobilians take pride in their surroundings. As this early-twentieth-century interior view of the home of Gregory M. Luce at 1363 Government Street suggests, there is in most cases an elegance inside as well as out. (Historic Mobile Preservation Society.)

Paying close attention to every detail of the entrance to their homes, many Mobilians clearly want their guests to feel welcome. The Marshall-Hixon house at 152 Tuthill Lane, completed in 1853, is one of Mobile's most stately residences. The iron gates open into a beautifully landscaped, circular drive around a large brick fountain with a reflecting pool. The broad steps, covered with slate, and Doric columns frame the double doors of the entrance. Below, the home of Dr. and Mrs. John Dae Peake, one of the most beautiful on McGregor Avenue, is set at the end of a spectacular brick drive. Jarvis red camellias line the entrance, offering a comfortable invitation to the home. (N.B. Gaillard.)

Confederate sea raider Raphael Semmes, regarded by the Union Navy as a pirate and by the people of Mobile as a hero, spent his later years in this house on Government Street. The house was built in 1848 and then in 1871 was bought for Semmes by the people of the city. On April 22, 1946, it was presented to the First Baptist Church of Mobile. (W.F. Gaillard.)

This antebellum house, which stands at 1906 Spring Hill Avenue, is one of the best-known in all of Mobile. It was built in 1855 for Judge John Bragg, brother of Civil War General Braxton Bragg. With its tall, slender columns, and detailed features, it is a mixture of Greek and Italianate styles. Acquired by the Mitchell family in 1925, the house is now open for public tours. (W.F. Gaillard.)

The Quigley House, pictured here, serves as the national headquarters for America's Junior Miss Pageant. Built in 1860 by George Gilmore, the house at 751 Government Street was owned for a time by Dr. Edmund Pendleton Gaines and then by the Quigleys, who sold it to the City in 1963. The young women below are preparing for a dance routine in one of the pageants, a kind of Miss America competition for high school seniors. One historian described the pageant as "something of a Senior Bowl for high school girls," offering some of the brightest young women in the country an opportunity to display their talents. (W.F. Gaillard, University of South Alabama Archives.)

Dauphin Island, a spit of sand in the mouth of Mobile Bay, was the site of one of the first French forts in the region—and later, Fort Gaines, which played a pivotal role in the Battle of Mobile Bay. In addition to its human history, the island is rich in natural history as well. The Audubon Bird Sanctuary is a 164-acre preserve of marshlands and forest, which represents the first landfall for migratory birds making the long flight across the Gulf of Mexico. (W.F. Gaillard.)

Wilmer Hall, at the foot of Spring Hill, is one of Mobile's most historic institutions. Built in 1864 and named in honor of Bishop Richard Wilmer, the colorful Episcopalian cleric, the Hall has provided a home for orphans, as well as other children who need a warm and stable place to stay. Still going strong more than 130 years from its founding, it offers a reminder of Mobile's compassion. (W.F. Gaillard.)

Much of Mobile's history is carved into stone—quite literally, in fact, in the old cemeteries that are scattered through the city. The oldest of those, the Church Street Cemetery, just behind the downtown public library, dates back to the early yellow fever epidemics. Magnolia and Pine Crest are not far behind, and the Spring Hill Cemetery, pictured here, offers, like the others, a peaceful retreat and a permanent reminder of Mobile's past. (W.F. Gaillard.)

The Confederate Rest Monument is one of the most historic spots in Mobile's historic Magnolia Cemetery. Matthew Lawler carved the ornate statue of a Confederate soldier in 1871 to mark the burial site of 1,100 war dead. After lightning damaged the upper part of the figure, the statue was placed on a pedestal base. Four additional monuments are located around the statue, and they are dedicated to the Alabama Artillery, the Mobile Cadets, the men who died on the submarine *Hunley*, and General Braxton Bragg, a Confederate commander at the Battle of Chickamauga. (Historic Mobile Preservation Society.)

Some people say it's the prettiest chapel in all of Mobile, more modest than some of the downtown churches, but with a dignity unsurpassed by the greatest cathedrals. "The little church," as it's known to the members of St. Paul's Episcopal, was consecrated in 1861. The church was known in its early years for its association with Bishop Richard Wilmer, one of Mobile's most respected clerics. He ministered there for thirty-five years, beginning near the end of the Civil War and continuing until the turn of the twentieth century. (W.F. Gaillard.)

The Visitation Convent and Academy, founded in 1833, served for almost 120 years as a Catholic school for girls, one of the fine educational centers in the South. Today, the convent on Spring Hill Avenue is a house of retreat for a small but committed order of sisters, who spend their days in work and prayer. (Historic Mobile Preservation Society.)

On December 8, 1850, Bishop Michael Portier consecrated the Cathedral of the Immaculate Conception, Mobile's historic basilica. The new cathedral was built for the oldest Catholic parish on the Gulf, established in 1704 with the Rev. Henri Roulleaux de la Vente as pastor. The building, with its austere entrance, holds a powerful beauty inside—an interplay of mahogany, stained glass, and marble. (W.F. Gaillard.)

In 1826, Mobile architect George B. Rogers created the Government Street United Methodist Church— "the Beehive," as many people called it. The nickname referred to the dedicated members who would "swarm" all over the community forming new congregations. The original wooden structure—the mother church for Mobile Methodists—was replaced by a brick sanctuary in 1848–49, and again in 1890 by the Gothic structure shown above. (W.F. Gaillard.)

Following the lead of the Methodists, Presbyterians, and Episcopalians, who established places of worship in the early 1800s, the members of First Baptist Church have been on a mission for Christ since 1835. Six large white columns spread across the entrance to the church at 806 Government Street, making it one of the most striking buildings in the city. (W.F. Gaillard.)

Now designated by the U.S. Department of the Interior as a national historic building, Government Street Presbyterian Church, with its elegant front styling and Corinthian interior, has been a Mobile landmark since 1836. Reverend John B. Warren founded the church with only twenty-one members. It has grown significantly since that time and remains today the Presbyterian mother church for southern Alabama. (W.F. Gaillard.)

The Creole Fire House on Dearborn Street, home of a volunteer fire company organized in 1819, was part of the social structure for Mobile's Creoles, or mixed blood citizens, who maintained their own schools, churches, and social organizations throughout the latter years of the nineteenth century. The old fire engines below are typical of those that are still on display at the Phoenix Fire Museum on South Claiborne Street, which was also the home of a volunteer fire company. (W.F. Gaillard, Southern Litho Co.)

Middle-class homes as well as mansions pay their tributes to Mobile's history. The house at the right is one of many in the city's garden district that add a touch of architectural class. The house below is part of Widow's Row, one in a group of neat, modest homes in the area around Eslava Street, built in the 1860s for widows. Many of these houses are now being restored. (W.F. Gaillard.)

One of Mobile's oldest plantation-style homes, the Toulmin house was built in 1828 by Theophilus Toulmin, a state legislator and Mobile postmaster. The exterior of the house has changed very little since the days when John Quincy Adams was president, but the structure has been restored and preserved by the University of South Alabama, which moved the house from a part of the city where its future was threatened, to take its handsome place on the campus. (W.F. Gaillard.)

This Gulf Coast cottage was built in 1836, just down the road from Spring Hill College. It is owned today by Julie Suk, a Mobile-born poet widely recognized as one of the best in the South. The picture was taken by S.P. Gaillard, a Mobile lawyer, who bought the house in 1903 as a present for his wife. (Gaillard family collection.)

Four
People

President Woodrow Wilson came to Mobile on October 27, 1913, and delivered one of the important speeches of his presidency. In an address before the Southern Commercial Congress, Wilson spoke of a new international order, and in eloquent and unmistakable terms he renounced imperialism as a cornerstone of American foreign policy. "The United States," he declared, "will never again seek one additional foot of territory by conquest." Wilson's speech and his visit to the city were part of a pattern in Mobile, which became accustomed through the years to receiving important guests from other places. The city also produced celebrities of its own—particularly men and women of letters and political leaders who left their marks. In the final analysis, the story of Mobile is the story of its people, some famous, some not, who have long been proud of their encounters with history. (Museum of Mobile.)

Another famous visitor to the city, General Le Marquis de Lafayette, arrived in Mobile in 1827 to ringing bells and booming cannon, all in his honor. The city thus extended its hospitality to the Revolutionary War hero during his tour of the newly liberated United States. (Whitlock, *Lafayette*, Vol. II, 1929; University of South Alabama Archives.)

Seen here in his trademark Panama hat, left foreground, Theodore Roosevelt addresses an expectant crowd in Bienville Square. Roosevelt visited Mobile in 1905, seeking to explore the city's ties to Latin America. His Panama Canal project was of particular interest to the commercial sector of Mobile, and the president, recently elected to his first full term, received a warm welcome from the city. (William E. Wilson Collection, Historic Mobile Preservation Society.)

Octavia Walton Le Vert served as the most influential societal diva in antebellum Mobile. Her salon became a magnet for the intellectual and social elite. Celebrities like General Lafayette, among many other notables, came there for hospitality and vivacious debate. Madame Le Vert, highly educated herself, did not hesitate to argue her own convictions, expressing distaste in her writings for the societal limitations on women. (University of South Alabama Archives.)

Admiral Raphael Semmes was one of Mobile's heroes, a swashbuckling Confederate sea raider who was born in Maryland and moved to Mobile after service in the Mexican War. He practiced law for a while but never lost his love of the sea, and when war broke out in 1861, he joined the service of the Confederate Navy. On his ship *Alabama*, he roamed the globe and terrorized the U.S. merchant fleet, until his boat was sunk off the coast of France, June 19, 1864. In the sketch shown here, Semmes was rescued by the *Deerhound*, a British pleasure boat. (Erik Overbey Collection of the University of South Alabama Archives; Museum of Mobile.)

John Gayle, an active participant in Alabama politics since territorial days, began his career as a state representative. He later became a justice of the state supreme court and then governor of Alabama. Gayle's years as governor were some of the most pivotal in the early history of the state. It was during that time in the 1830s that Alabama sought the removal of the Creek Indians to a reservation west of the Mississippi River, and when states' rights sentiments began to take hold, laying the groundwork for secession. In the courtroom pictured here, Gayle served as a federal judge from 1848–1858, the eve of the war that now seemed inevitable. (Historic Mobile Preservation Society.)

A magisterial presence with his robes and flowing beard, Bishop Richard Wilmer was concentrated under the Episcopal Church, C.S.A., as the denomination was known during the years of the Confederacy, 1861–1865. In the Reconstruction era that followed, Bishop Wilmer remained fiercely loyal to the South. He refused to allow his Episcopal congregations to pray for the president of the United States, so long as Federal troops were still in Mobile. Those troops, in response, closed down the churches until President Andrew Johnson overruled their decision. In addition to stirring political controversy, Wilmer was a founder of the Mobile Infirmary and a Mobile orphanage that still bears his name. (Alabama Department of Archives and History, University of South Alabama Archives.)

One of the most important sons of Mobile and one of the greatest physicians of his time, William Crawford Gorgas served as surgeon-general in the United States Army. In 1904, he was appointed sanitary officer in the Panama Canal Zone, where he set about cleaning out the mosquito-breeding area that was known to be the source of yellow fever and malaria. Without his work, it is almost certain that the Panama Canal could not have been built. (Alabama Department of Archives and History.)

In the early 1900s, many black women worked as domestics, but Lillian Thomas had other dreams. Educated at Emerson Institute and Talladega College, she used her talents to become a missionary to the Congo, sponsored for a time by the all-white Government Street Presbyterian Church. She believed in the power of an education, as well as the power of the Christian faith, and those were the driving forces of her work. (Museum of the City of Mobile.)

As Mobile's most famous literary figure until her death in 1909, Augusta Evans Wilson might be considered the Danielle Steel of her day. She was more Victorian than her modern counterpart, but equally as popular by the standards of the nineteenth century. She wrote eight novels, including *Vashti* and *Inez: A Tale of the Alamo*, and her best-seller, *St. Elmo*, was later made into a silent film. Two of her Civil War-era novels were highly effective as Confederate propaganda. The critics were often hard on her work— "affectation run mad," one of them wrote—but the public was taken with her romantic plots, filled with moralism and propriety. (Gaillard family collection.)

Once a Princeton classmate of Woodrow Wilson and a successful Mobile lawyer, Peter J. Hamilton earned his greatest acclaim as a writer. His book, *Colonial Mobile*, still holds a place as a definitive and well-crafted study of Mobile's history. Hamilton's personal and academic abilities did not go unnoticed in his lifetime. In 1913, President Wilson appointed him to a federal judgeship in Puerto Rico. (Erik Overbey Collection, University of South Alabama Archives.)

John Forsyth, one of Mobile's most notable antebellum intellectuals, served as editor of the *Mobile Register* for twenty years. He was also, in the course of his career, minister to Mexico, mayor of Mobile, and commissioner to Washington for the Confederate government. Forsyth was a regular at Madame Le Vert's salon (see page 67) for the rounds of political and intellectual debate. (Historic Mobile Preservation Society.)

The Apache war chief Geronimo stares fiercely from a postcard on sale in Mobile. After their surrender in 1886, Geronimo and his band were shipped by train to military camps in the East—first to Florida and then to Mount Vernon Barracks in Mobile County. The Apache didn't like the dense pine forests along the Mobile River, as they missed the sun and the wide-open spaces. Some of them became so morose that they climbed to the tops of trees to see the sky. Geronimo spent seven years in Mobile County, a time full of heartache and alien disease, before his people were granted a reservation in the West. (Frank Randall, Leib Image Archives, York, PA.)

Louis Augustus Herpin posed as a proud veteran and the last survivor of the Battle of Mobile Bay. The photograph was made in front of the Herpin home on Franklin Street in Mobile. Like many other young men in the South, Herpin was eager to serve, and he joined the Confederate Army when he was sixteen. He died in his nineties, shortly after this photograph was made. (Erik Overbey Collection, University of South Alabama Archives.)

Joe Cain, shown here in his Indian costume, is credited with the founding of Mobile's Mardi Gras in 1866. A market clerk and roustabout town wit, Cain dressed himself as Chief Slackabamirimico from Wragg Swamp and paraded through the streets playing music. Each Shrove Tuesday thereafter, more and more people joined the parade, and Mobile's mystic societies were born. (University of South Alabama Archives.)

Documentary photographer William E. Wilson operated a Mobile studio from 1894 and through the early years of the twentieth century. Compared by some to the Civil War photographer Matthew Brady, Wilson set out to document a vanishing way of life, as well as the New South he saw all around him. He left behind more than 2,000 glass negatives— "a treasure trove," in the words of one Mobile historian—and many examples of his work appear in this book. (William E. Wilson Collection, Historic Mobile Preservation Society.)

The egalitarian eye of William Wilson's camera is clear on this page. In the picture to the right, an elderly black woman appears to be alone with her thoughts, her eyes averted from the stare of the camera. Below, a young white woman in a slightly cluttered room searches out a melody on her piano. The names of the subjects have since been lost. Their humanity, however, has been preserved, their dignity apparent a hundred years after the photographs were taken. (William E. Wilson Collection, Historic Mobile Preservation Society.)

These two William E. Wilson photographs offer contrasting images of life in Mobile, one of leisure, the other of work. In the photo above, Miss Zemma Mastin poses with her pony and buggy in front of her house on Government Street. Note the feminine touch—a buggy whip adorned with a bow. In the photo below, marble workers take a break from their grueling tasks to pose for a picture. In this plant, as in other settings early in the century, blacks and whites worked side by side, though all were aware of the invisible lines that were dangerous to cross. (Historic Mobile Preservation Society.)

James Reese Europe, a Mobile native, was a music pioneer whose Clef Club Orchestra in 1912 became the first black band to play Carnegie Hall. Some of the musicians who played with Europe went on to distinguished careers in jazz, citing his influence on their music. The bandleader himself never quite reached his musical potential. He was murdered in Boston in 1919, stabbed in the throat by a deranged member of his band. Before that happened, he was honored for his bravery in World War I, where he became the first black officer to serve in the trenches. He also worked as a union organizer who fought for equal employment opportunities and fairer pay for African-American musicians. (Maryland Historical Society.)

Choctaw Indians once lived on the shores of Mobile County, near the town of Coden. Under the leadership of Chief Pushmataha, the tribe fought on the side of Andrew Jackson in the Creek Indian War of 1813. These impoverished survivors of a once proud culture were captured on film by photographer William E. Wilson. His out-of-focus image, intentionally or not, suggests a disappearing way of life in the troubled, early years of the twentieth century. (William E. Wilson Collection, Historic Mobile Preservation Society.)

Against all the odds, there are still Choctaws in Mobile County, and their culture and identity are getting stronger all the time. Under the leadership of Chief Wilford Longhair Taylor, pictured at right, the tribe presented a powerful petition in 1996 to be officially recognized by the federal government—a status that Taylor and others believe could help usher in a new era of progress for their people. (Carolyn DeMeritt.)

John LeFlore, Mobile's preeminent civil rights leader, is shown here in 1969 after being arrested at America's Junior Miss Pageant. LeFlore had taken no part in the demonstrations outside the pageant, and according to one newspaper account, he was arrested simply because he was there. He was known to most of Mobile's citizens as one of the stalwarts in the push for equal rights. Born in 1911, he joined the NAACP in 1925, and worked for voting rights and integration. In 1965, shots were fired at his house in Mobile, and two years later his home was bombed. LeFlore, however, simply kept pushing. In the late 1960s, a time of scattered racial violence, LeFlore stood firm for the cause of non-violence, and there were blacks who criticized his moderation, even though many whites still viewed him as extreme. Today, at last, his memory is honored by a local high school that carries his name. (University of South Alabama Archives.)

Joe Langan, former Mobile mayor, was another voice for racial moderation. During his thirty-year political career, which began in 1939, Langan increased employment opportunities for blacks, especially in Mobile's police and fire departments, and during the troubled years of the 1960s, he set up a biracial committee to pursue the desegregation of lunch counters. Some historians argue that he and John LeFlore (see previous page) helped create a climate of calm that was unique among the major cities in the state. (University of South Alabama Archives.)

The Rev. Jesse Jackson, second from the left, posed with several of Mobile's black leaders. On the far left is John LeFlore, and on the far right is Robert Lucy. Towering over the group is Gary Cooper, later named U.S. Ambassador to Jamaica. Not pictured is Cooper's brother, A.J., who, in 1972, became the first black mayor of Prichard, the second-largest city in Mobile County. (University of South Alabama Archives.)

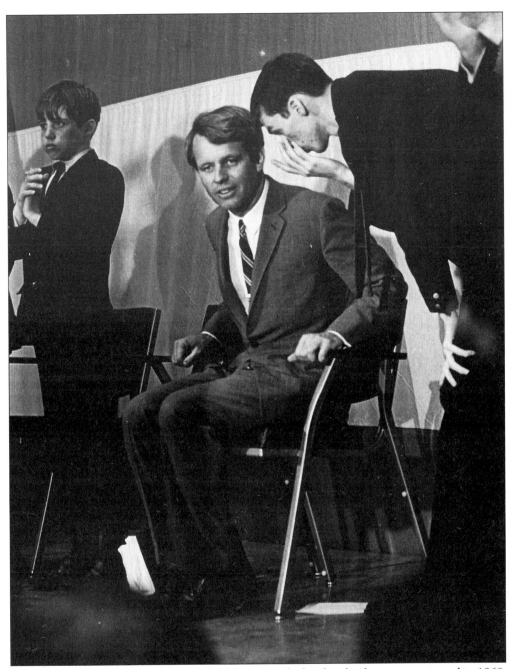

When Robert F. Kennedy, who visited Alabama just before his death, was assassinated in 1968, Mobile songwriter Dick Holler was one of millions who were stricken by the loss. Until that time, Holler had written mostly lighter fare—songs such as "Snoopy vs. the Red Baron." But with the death of Kennedy, he sat down and wrote a haunting tribute called "Abraham, Martin and John." The song, soon recorded by Dion DiMucci, captures powerfully and simply the grief and idealism of the 1960s. (Gaillard family collection.)

Popular singer/songwriter Jimmy Buffet made his childhood home in Mobile. According to Buffet's personal testimony, regular visits to the Dew Drop Inn fostered his love of cheeseburgers, and thus the inspiration for his hit single, "Cheeseburger in Paradise." (Sunshine Smith, MCA Records.)

Of all Mobile's men of letters in the twentieth century, the best known has to be Winston Groom, now a resident of Point Clear. His classic book, *Forrest Gump*, which is set in part in Mobile County, offers a funny and poignant look back at the social upheavals of the 1960s and the changes in the country in the years after that. (Tom Corcoran, courtesy of Pocket Books.)

Five
Playgrounds to the Hall of Fame

Crouched on an imaginary 50-yard line, these Mobile youngsters reflect a city-wide enthusiasm for the world of sports. Aspiring young athletes from the Bay area never lacked for heroes, as greats like Henry Aaron and Satchel Paige proved that a humble Mobile beginning could actually be an asset in a drive for the big leagues. Mobile County boasts four members in baseball's Hall of Fame, as well as two members of the team still referred to as "the Miracle Mets." Here, the legendary Bear Bryant coached his first football game for the University of Alabama, Willie McCovey first picked up a bat, and Ken Stabler, who played across the bay in Foley, first dazzled scouts as a high school quarterback. They were not alone, with more professional players and stars preceding them, and more still likely to come. Asked to explain what made Mobile such a fertile ground for sports heroes, Billy Williams, himself a baseball Hall of Famer, could only offer this explanation: "There must be something in the water down there." (Erik Overbey Collection, University of South Alabama Archives.)

Greeted by broadcaster Bill Menton on a return visit to their native Mobile, major leaguers Hank Aaron (right) and Billy Williams (left) enjoy a break between seasons. At the age of sixteen, Aaron was discovered by major league scouts playing fast-pitch softball at Carver Park, where he batted in an awkward cross-handed style. They cured him of that, and by the time his professional career was over, he had broken Babe Ruth's home run record, hitting 755, while also setting the major league record for RBI's. He was elected to the Baseball Hall of Fame, as was his friend, Billy Williams, a native of the Mobile County town of Whistler. Williams got his start hitting bottle caps with broomsticks. Eventually, he played for eighteen years in the major leagues, sixteen of those for the Chicago Cubs. He hit 426 home runs. (University of South Alabama Archives.)

WILLIE MC COVEY

Willie McCovey, one of the National League's greatest home run hitters, is one of four Hall of Fame baseball players who grew up on the sandlots of Mobile County. Throughout his career, McCovey was admired for his work ethic as well as his talent. He hit 521 home runs and won recognition as one of the best defensive first basemen in the game. (San Francisco Giants.)

No one knows for sure when Leroy "Satchel" Paige was born, but it was apparently sometime around 1906. He got his nickname from a boyhood job in which he carried bags at the L & N railroad station in Mobile. About the same time, he was sent to reform school for stealing jewelry, but it was there that he learned the game of baseball. Because of racial segregation, he spent his prime, twenty-two years, in the Negro Leagues before signing with the Cleveland Indians in 1948. He played five seasons with the Indians, then retired. But in 1965, as a gimmick intended to attract more fans, the last-place Kansas City Athletics invited Paige to pitch in one of their games. At the astonishing age of at least 59, he pitched three scoreless innings and struck out a batter. It was a reminder of what he must have been in his prime—a greatness that allowed him, in 1971, to be elected to baseball's Hall of Fame. (University of South Alabama Archives.)

Almost everyone who followed baseball in 1969 agreed on one thing: The New York Mets were destined to have a disastrous season. After finishing ninth in the previous year, they began with a young, inexperienced ball club, with Cleon Jones (left) and Tommy Agee (right) of Mobile representing two of a handful of veterans on the roster. To the astonishment of the nation, however, the Mets not only began to win, but went on to make the playoffs. The fielding of Agee and the hitting of Jones contributed heavily to the team's turnaround. The Mobilians were stars in the National League championship games against Atlanta, and they helped push the Mets into the World Series. There, in what many observers said was a miracle, the Mets beat Baltimore four games to one. (New York Mets.)

In 1969, Amos Otis, another major league star from Mobile, also played for the New York Mets. A second-year player, Otis hit only .151, but better days were ahead. Otis played seventeen years in the major leagues, and was one of the heroes of the 1980 World Series. (Kansas City Royals.)

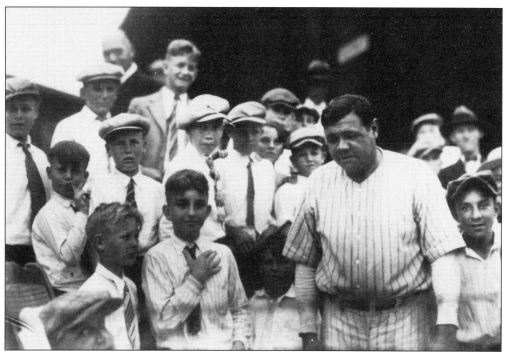

The great Babe Ruth, shown here with his most avid fans, made several appearances in Mobile. The earliest of those came at Monroe Park, the city's playground down by the bay. Later, he appeared at Hartwell Field, where his New York Yankees beat their Rochester farm team 8–2 in an exhibition game. Ruth ended his legendary career with 714 home runs, now second all-time to Mobile's Henry Aaron. (Erik Overbey Collection, University of South Alabama Archives.)

It's out at third on another close play at Monroe Park, home of both professional and amateur baseball from the turn of the century to 1926. In 1924, Babe Ruth hit a home run at the park, past the wood-frame center field fence, but most of those who played at Monroe—for teams with names like the Mobile Sea Gulls—were not quite as famous or proficient as the Babe. The competition, however, was no less keen. (William E. Wilson Collection, Historic Mobile Preservation Society.)

Baseball was a game for the masses in the years just after the turn of the century. Always a spectator sport, it also offered opportunities for amateurs who wanted to feel the crack of the bat in their hands. In the team portrait above and the ragged newspaper photo below, these unidentified players clearly take pride in being part of a team. (William E. Wilson Collection, Historic Mobile Preservation Society.)

The Class AA Mobile Bears were the pride of the city in 1947, when they won the Southern League championship. One of the stars on the team (back row, third from the left) was Chuck Connors, who later went on to fame as an actor in the television show, *The Rifleman*. Through the years, the Bears also produced their share of major leaguers, including Ty Cline, Gordy Coleman, and Jim Gentile. The teams have played in several different homes: Monroe Park, Hartwell Field (below), and now in the 1990s, the 6,000-seat Hank Aaron Stadium. (Erik Overbey Collection, University of South Alabama Archives; Mobile Municipal Archives.)

Eddie "the Brat" Stanky vigorously denies the accuracy of his nickname. The former major leaguer, now living in Fairhope, says he played the game "as hard as anybody," but with a high regard for sportsmanship and fairness. As coach at the University of South Alabama, where the baseball field is named in his honor, he expected the same of his players. The formula worked. Stanky appeared in the World Series and four All-Star games, and in 1972 he coached the South Alabama Jaguars to the national championship. (University of South Alabama Archives.)

Here, South Alabama's 1972 national championship team poses beside the team bus. In Eddie Stanky's fourteen years as coach, 1969–1983, the Jaguars emerged as a national power. (University of South Alabama Archives.)

It's halftime at the Senior Bowl, Mobile's premier sporting event. The all-star game for the nation's best college seniors began its life in Jacksonville, Florida, where, in 1950, the crowd was so sparse for the inaugural game that many people thought it was a flash in the pan. The following year, however, the game was moved to Mobile at the behest of a group of local businessmen that included Ralph Chandler, publisher of the Mobile Press Register, and Finley McRae, CEO at Merchants National Bank. Over the past forty years, some of football's greatest stars have played in the game, including Dan Marino, Terry Bradshaw, and Bubba Smith. (University of South Alabama Archives.)

On September 27, 1958, Paul "Bear" Bryant made his debut as head football coach at the University of Alabama. His first game (see picture below) was played at Mobile's Ladd Memorial Stadium, and even though it ended in a loss—13–3 to national champion LSU—it was clear that better days were ahead. The year before, Alabama had won only two games and had lost 40–0 to arch-rival Auburn. By 1961, Bryant won his first national championship at Alabama, and emerged as a folk hero in the state. He prowled the sidelines in his hound's tooth hat, his teams invariably played hard and clean, and he won more games than any other major college coach. Many Mobilians are proud of the fact that the Bear Bryant legend began in their city. (Paul W. Bryant Museum.)

These two number 12's—Kenny Stabler (right) and Scott Hunter (below)—played high school football in the Mobile area, Stabler at Foley and Hunter at Vigor. Both went on to stardom at the University of Alabama, and both later played in the NFL. Hunter, shown handing off to Johnny Musso, quarterbacked for the Green Bay Packers, and Stabler was a star for the Oakland Raiders. Another Mobile quarterback, Richard Todd, also played at Alabama and then professionally for the New York Jets. (Paul W. Bryant Museum.)

Mobilian Paul Crane played linebacker in the 1960s on Alabama's national championship team, then played for the Super Bowl champion New York Jets. When his playing days were over, Crane returned to his hometown to become the football coach at McGill-Toolen High School. (Paul W. Bryant Museum.)

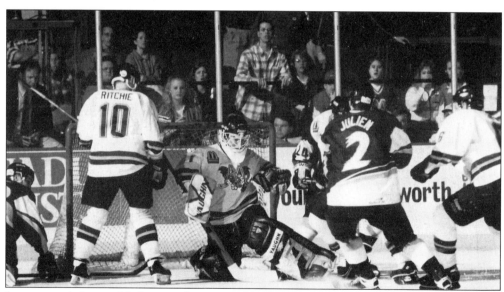

In a part of the world that revolves around summer, ice hockey historically has been an afterthought. But it appears to have caught on now with the Mobile Mysticks, a professional hockey team that has emerged as a championship contender in its league. From Louisiana to North Carolina, the sport has gained popularity in the South, and Mobile has been a part of that trend. (Mike Marti, courtesy of Mobile Mysticks Hockey Club.)

Doug Barfield, athletic director at the University of Mobile, has made his greatest mark through the years as a high school coach—one of the best that Mobile has ever seen. In the 1960s, he led the football team at UMS, a small private school, to three consecutive county championships, compiling a record of 25–5 against the largest public schools in the area. Later, he became head coach at Auburn, where his winning record was matched by his reputation for integrity. (University of Mobile.)

John Stimpson, the best tennis player Mobile has produced, was an All-American at the University of Alabama before embarking on a pro career that led him to the qualifying rounds at Wimbledon, the French Open, and the U.S. Open. In the course of his career, he beat such future stars as Jim Courier and MalaVai Washington. (Courtesy Nedra Stimpson.)

Not all competitors set out to be stars. Here on the shores of Mobile Bay, a group of amateur golfers in the early 1900s enjoy what appears to be a leisurely round. The course, located not far from Monroe Park on the Mobile County side of the Bay, was destroyed by the hurricane of 1906. Until that time, it offered a peaceful retreat for those with the time and the patience for the game. (Historic Mobile Preservation Society.)

Six
The Eastern Shore

On June, 15, 1927, the causeway opened across Mobile Bay, providing a new and convenient link between Mobile County and the Eastern Shore. The opening led to quite a traffic jam, as the cars lined up to make the trip, and Alabama Governor Bibb Graves led a host of dignitaries who were there to celebrate. The string of bridges spanning the shallow headwaters of the Bay, as well as the Mobile and Tensaw Rivers, was the brainchild of Mobile Mayor Harry Hartwell and businessman John Cochrane, president of the Alabama, Tennessee, and Northern Railroad. The causeway, endorsed by leaders from Jacksonville, Florida, to San Diego, California, was seen as another vital link in a Southern transcontinental highway. More immediately, it strengthened the bond between Mobile and the smaller communities of Baldwin County, most of which had rich histories of their own. (Erik Overbey Collection, University of South Alabama Archives.)

Carrying passengers from Fairhope to Mobile, *The Bay Queen* was one of the most luxurious ships to visit either port. The trip across Mobile Bay was about 15 miles and lasted a little over an hour. Until the causeway was built, ending the need for its service, this ship, as well as others, gave families and vacationers a pleasant way to make the journey. The Slosson family, whose car has been unloaded below, actually lived in an apartment in Mobile during the week so that the children could attend school and music classes, but the family then returned to Fairhope for the weekends. (Pinky Bass Collection, Lois Slosson Sundberg Collection.)

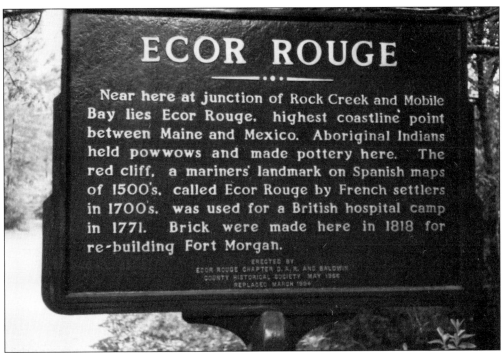

This historic bluff on the eastern shore of Mobile Bay, once a gathering spot for Native Americans and a landmark for the earliest European explorers, is currently a part of the community of Montrose. Now landscaped for beachfront homes, most of the shoreline is no longer as dramatic, but it still retains much of its scenic appeal. (W.F. Gaillard.)

Some using ropes, others simply scrambling hand over hand, a group of schoolchildren from Fairhope scale the cliffs on Mobile Bay. Along with their teachers (bottom right), most have stopped in the middle of their climb to pose for the camera of turn-of-the-century photographer Frank Stewart.

Described by a Battles Wharf old-timer as "a crazy bunch of Yankees with a crazy idea," these gentlemen were some of the founders of the Fairhope Single Tax Colony. They came to Fairhope to form a model community that was free from all forms of private monopoly. They believed that "land is a free gift of nature; that all men have an equal right to the use of the land." Twenty-eight individuals, including children, comprised the original settlers, coming from as far as Missouri and Nebraska. The most influential was E.B. Gaston, whose vision was at the heart of the Fairhope experiment. (Fairhope Single Tax Corporation.)

Fairhope just after the turn of the century was beginning to grow, but it was still a far cry from the handsome community it would later become, graced by a canopy of live oak trees. This photograph, taken sometime after 1915, shows the view from the Fairhope water tower. (Frank Stewart.)

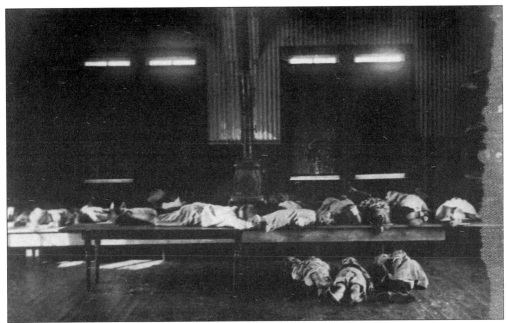

In the photo above, it's naptime at the Organic School. In the village of Fairhope, the school was founded in 1907 and attracted students from all over the world because of its unique educational philosophy. Under the leadership of Marietta Johnson, students learned through real life experiences designed to develop the "whole child." The wood-frame building that once housed the school (photo below) is now a part of the Fairhope Campus of Faulkner State College. (Frank Stewart.)

A rustic, one-room schoolhouse served the permanent population of the community of Point Clear in the early years of the twentieth century. This scenic area on the shores of the bay, just south of Fairhope, emerged as a popular vacation spot. Until recent years, however, the number of year-round residents was small. (William E. Wilson Collection, Historic Mobile Preservation Society.)

The Point Clear Hotel, a fashionable resort at the turn of the century, is pictured here just before the hurricane of 1906—one of the great cataclysms in the history of the Bay. The hotel was restored, as it had been after other disasters in its history, and it remains today one of the South's most elegant destinations for travelers. (William E. Wilson Collection, Historic Mobile Preservation Society.)

Before the Civil War, many slaves attended church with their masters, most often segregated in the balcony. After emancipation, the first order of business was frequently to establish a church of their own—a symbol of their newfound freedom and pride. Such was the case for Little Bethel Baptist Church in Daphne, where industrious members like Russell Dick, now buried in the cemetery out back, struggled heroically to build new lives for themselves and their families. (W.F. Gaillard.)

A pensive dignity and pride are clear in the bearing of Minerva Hill, a domestic worker in the town of Silverhill, pictured here in a front-porch rocker. The photograph was taken early in the twentieth century by Lois Slosson Sundberg, one of Baldwin County's most gifted documentary photographers.

Even at the end of the twentieth century, much of Baldwin County is farming country, and many of its residents, including those a generation removed, remember scenes like the ones pictured here. In the photograph above, members of the Sundberg family pose on the porch of their home in Silverhill. Below, a pair of farmworkers pause in the midst of the task of shearing sheep. (Lois Slosson Sundberg.)

The names of these Baldwin County families are now unknown, but their neighbor, Lois Slosson Sundberg, set out to capture their rural lifestyle, as well as their shy and curious personalities. In the photograph below, in addition to those who have posed more formally, children are peeking out the door at the camera. Sundberg, who had no formal photographic training, nevertheless had a feel for the life and the character of the region where she lived. (Lois Slosson Sundberg.)

In this photograph from the turn of the century, a Baldwin County woman poses with her cow, who had taken on the status of the family pet. The windmill and sturdy wood-frame buildings in the background suggest an air of self-sufficiency and pride that the photographer found among many of her neighbors. (Lois Slosson Sundberg.)

Lois Sundberg's gift as a portrait photographer is clear in this elegant shot of her relative, Nell Slosson, shown on the porch of her Baldwin County house, with a feline friend nestled in her lap. Nell Slosson was blind, but didn't let it stop her. She played the piano and violin, raised singing canaries, and sang at churches and social events in the county. (Lois Slosson Sundberg.)

Frank Stewart, the Picture Man, moved to Silverhill in the mid-1890s where he first tried his hand at farming. Although he was blind in one eye, he became fascinated by lights and shadows and took up photography. He traveled the back roads making photographs, moved to Fairhope in 1914, and opened the Fairhope Photo Shop.

Frank Stewart is pictured here "giving postcards a final bath" in Pole Creek in the town of Silverhill. Curiously, what was believed to be tannic acid in the water acted as a natural preservative for the photographic cards. (Frank Stewart Collection, University of South Alabama Archives.)

This group of men, all of whom fought for the North during the Civil War, gathered in Baldwin County for a reunion early in the 1900s. One member of the group, Ed Slosson, was wounded at the Battle of Blakeley outside of Mobile, shortly after Lee's surrender at Appomattox. (Pinky Bass Collection.)

During the 1930s, the era of the Big Bands, there were abundant opportunities for local musicians. This group of residents from the Eastern Shore—male and female, young and old—formed the Baldwin County Student Orchestra, providing entertainment for local events. (Frank Stewart Collection.)

The Peoples' Railroad, which served the community for more than ten years, was a dream of one of Fairhope's founders, E.B. Gaston. Originally, the railroad was to be a full-service train connecting Fairhope's wharf, via Silverhill, with the existing railroad going through Robertsdale. Like some of Fairhope's other projects that never materialized, this one fell far short of its goal. Only one mile of the proposed fourteen was ever completed. Beginning in 1912, however, the train served in effect as a Fairhope trolley. (Fairhope Single Tax Corporation.)

The community water pump, pictured here in 1897, was located in the center of the Fairhope Avenue and Section Street intersection. In 1915, it was replaced by a water tank, where the town's water supply is still located. (Pinky Bass Collection.)

Here, Dr. Edwin Slosson, a homeopathic physician in Fairhope who was known to his patients simply as Doc, drives the first automobile in the town. Doc Slosson, who came to Fairhope in 1907, thought the vehicle was so unique that he gave it a name, the Sarah Jane. According to a story handed down in the family, when he bought the car it had no brakes, and in order to stop it, he was forced to circle the yard until his brother Gene in the seat beside him was finally able to lasso a tree. (Lois Slosson Sundberg.)

Beneath a canopy of live oak trees, Doc Slosson, one of Fairhope's leading citizens, holds his granddaughter, Marion Sundberg. Slosson was one of those who was drawn to the town, in part at least, because of the idealism of its founders. (Lois Slosson Sundberg.)

The Jackson Oak, one of the Eastern Shore's favorite picnic spots, was a place of special beauty with the Spanish moss streaming from its outstretched limbs. As one visitor to Baldwin County remarked, "When God made trees, everything was just practice until he came to the live oak." (Frank Stewart Collection.)

Ever since its founding, Fairhope has offered a wide array of cultural opportunities. In the early years, women's clubs met regularly and gave their members a chance to be active in civic life. These young women, so fashionably dressed, were members of the Non-Pareil Club, which met regularly to hear lectures, musical renditions, and readings. (Frank Stewart Collection.)

The catch of the day is on display by the these two proud fishermen from the Eastern Shore. At least in the early 1900s, catfish grew large in the ponds and streams of Baldwin County, and the frying pan was waiting back home. (Lois Slosson Sundberg.)

Fish River, whose calm, dark waters make their unhurried way to the bay, has long been a stream that lives up to its name. Shortly after the turn of the century, these two fisherman in their small wooden skiff caught the attention of a Baldwin County photographer. (Lois Slosson Sundberg.)

The courthouse in Bay Minette became, in 1901, the third seat of government in Baldwin County—but not without the help of the town's determined residents. The original site, according to legend, was in Blakeley, at the base of a large oak tree. The judge, it is said, presided over sessions while sitting in the branches. When yellow fever wiped out Blakeley, Daphne became the new county seat. At the turn of the century, the Alabama legislature moved the seat again, this time to Bay Minette, but the residents of Daphne refused to give up their center of government. In response, a group of Bay Minette citizens converged on Daphne and took the records in a bloodless coup. Nearly one hundred years later, Bay Minette remains the seat of county government. (Pinky Bass Collection.)

In the picture above, family members gather on the front porch of the W.B. Curran house in the community of Battles Wharf, just north of Point Clear. Expansive porches like the one shown here were a common sight along Mobile Bay, a concession to the hot Southern climate, built for the breezes blowing in from the water. The Moog residence below, home to a turn-of-the-century merchant, also features an inviting front porch and shuttered windows as a protection against storms moving in from the Gulf. (The William E. Wilson Collection, Historic Mobile Preservation Society.)

The oak-covered grounds of the Grand Hotel have helped to make it one of the most exclusive resorts in the country. Built on the shores of Mobile Bay in a residential community known as Point Clear, the hotel has been a fixture since 1820. It has seen its share of adventures through the years, serving as a Confederate hospital in the 1860s and a training base for amphibious landings during World War II. It burned in 1875 and endured hurricanes in the twentieth century, but was rebuilt with its beauty and grace intact. (W.F. Gaillard.)

The stunning beauty of the Eastern Shore is captured here on the bluffs overlooking the Fairhope wharf. Because of such scenery, and also because of its history and climate, Fairhope has become a popular spot for artists and for part-time residents, seeking escape from the harsh winters of the North. It is still the heart of the Eastern Shore. (W.F. Gaillard.)

Seven
Changes

Two faces of Mobile, the old and the new, are clear in this picture. The brick building in the foreground, c. 1859, houses the Phoenix Fire Museum, former home of a volunteer fire company. In the background is the modernistic home of Mobile government, a building criticized by some as being out of place in historic downtown, but praised by others as a breath of architectural fresh air. Both are part of the same major effort to revitalize downtown Mobile, helping its history live on in the present. The effort has been led by Mayor Michael Dow, who, in the words of Mobile historian John Sledge, sees historic preservation as a key to the future. "A lot was lost in the 1960's," says Sledge. "Fortunately, we have so much. I think we've learned from our mistakes." (W.F. Gaillard)

The iron balconies of these old storefronts offer a sharp contrast to the glass of Mobile's new convention center. The ironwork of the old buildings has been a definitive feature of local architecture since the early nineteenth century. Much of the cast iron came from local manufacturers, as Mobile housed over a dozen foundries. Though the new convention center uses little of the city's decorative tradition, it does reflect a concern for the past. It was built on the historic waterfront, drawing people to the area for recreation and commerce, and reaffirming the heart of Mobile's identity. (Historic Mobile Preservation Society, W.F. Gaillard.)

Mobile's finest hotel in the 1850s, the original Battle House was destroyed by fire in 1905. Rebuilt as the new Battle House in 1908, it was a place for the wealthy and discerning to stay. Today, the future is uncertain for this old hotel, an elegant reminder of Mobile's past, though serious efforts are being made to save it. The same is true for the former G M & O railroad station (below), which sits empty on the edge of Mobile's waterfront. The hope has been that it can be restored as a transportation center, a home base for buses and taxis and trains. (William E. Wilson Collection, Historic Mobile Preservation Society.)

Arguably one of the most beautiful locations that Mobile offers, Bienville Square had a humble beginning. It was once the site of a livery stable where people flocked to watch the gamecock fights, most often held on the second floor. It was not until just before the Civil War that the square achieved its present dignified status. It was then that the area was landscaped, with the centerpiece being the live oak trees that offer their serenity and shelter even now. (Historic Mobile Preservation Society.)

Built between 1837 and 1840 as the U.S. Marine Hospital, this building now serves as the Mobile County Health Department. The hospital treated both Union and Confederate soldiers during the Civil War, and it later became the Sixth District Tuberculosis Hospital. (Historic Mobile Preservation Society.)

Mobile has long been known for its beautiful homes, many of them antebellum estates. But these two pictures show a different side of Mobile's heritage and another whole dimension of historic preservation. The home to the right is one of the remaining shotgun houses in the Oakleigh Garden District, several of which are being restored through the Mobile Revolving Fund for Historic Properties. Below is a finished home on Dearborn Street, not far from the Alabama Regional Planning Commission, a welcome addition to a revitalized downtown. (W.F. Gaillard.)

The Dew Drop Inn has changed on the outside since its founding by restauranteur George Widney in 1924, but the food has remained remarkably the same. It is believed to be the first Mobile establishment to serve, shortly after its founding, a revolutionary new sandwich known as the hot dog. In the years since then, its hamburgers, oyster loaves, and assorted other low-cost fare have made it an institution—spruced up slightly, but as distinctive today as when it first opened. (W.F. Gaillard.)

Wintzell's Oyster House, known for its friendly and unpretentious atmosphere, is a landmark in downtown Mobile. The restaurant stands on the corner of Dauphin and Warren Streets, in a building constructed in 1891 by Charles Peters and his brother Mason, who overcame a segregated society to become successful black entrepreneurs. (W.F. Gaillard.)

For 50¢ a copy, the citizens of this history-conscious community can find a lively and well-written entry point to the past. Cover stories like the one shown here, documenting the role of black Alabamians in the Civil War, are typical of the surprising array of articles. This small and unpretentious magazine, which seems to waste little time on the trimmings, has become a history buff's delight—one more illustration of the city's fascination with its past. (Courtesy of Old Mobile.)

More than twenty years ago, when Henry Aaron was pursuing Babe Ruth's legendary home run record, he often felt neglected by his hometown of Mobile, his race still a barrier in the minds of many citizens. Today, however, his legacy is embraced. The highway loop around the edge of downtown bears his name, as does the city's new baseball stadium. (W.F. Gaillard.)

The old becomes new at the Alabama School of Mathematics and Science (left) in downtown Mobile. This innovative educational program is housed in the former home of a mega-church, whose congregation left the city years ago for the suburbs. In the photo below, a junior high school, once old and tired, has been transformed into a public prep school—one of Mobile's magnets aimed at keeping the public school system strong. (W.F. Gaillard.)

Enjoying a slow, deliberate waddle across Old Shell Road, these ducks could afford a more leisurely pace at the turn of the century than they could today. In this photograph, they are the dirt road's only traffic, sheltered by live oak trees and a less hurried pace in Mobile. Today, the street is still in existence, a major east-west artery, and one of the busier roadways in the city. But some things never change. The same live oaks still offer their shade—stately reminders of Mobile's past, which lives on today, even as the community continues to change. (Historic Mobile Preservation Society.)

Acknowledgments

In putting together this book, we have benefited from the work and the assistance of many other people. Thanks first of all to the people at the Historic Mobile Preservation Society, particularly John Sledge and Jean Wentworth, and the University of South Alabama Archives, especially Lisa Baldwin and Michael Thomason. Thanks also to the Museum of the City of Mobile, the Mobile Public Library, the *Mobile Press Register*, the Paul W. Bryant Museum, the Maryland Historical Society, the Fairhope Single Tax Colony, and the Mobile Mysticks Hockey Club.

Among other sources we relied on were the following:
Mobile: The Life and Times of a Great Southern City, by Melton McLaurin and Michael Thomason; *Fairhope: 1894–1994 A Pictorial History*, by Larry Allums; *Man and Mission: E.B. Gaston and the Origins of the Fairhope Single Tax Colony*, by Paul M. Gaston; *The World Book Encyclopedia*; *Old Mobile Photograph Album*, published by First Federal Savings and Loan; *Bits of Charm*, by S. Blake McNeely; *Mobile: Fact and Tradition*, by Erwin Craighead; *The Athelston Club, A History*, published in 1979; *Glimpses of Old Mobile*, by Marian Acker Macpherson; *Alabama: The History of a Deep South State*, published by the University of Alabama Press; *Iron Ore to Iron Lace*, by Emily S. Van Antwerp; *Trying Times*, by Michael V.R. Thomason; *Once They Moved Like the Wind*, by David Roberts; *The Civil War: A Narrative*, by Shelby Foote; *Architectural History of Conde Charlotte House*, by Nicholas H. Holmes; *Nineteenth Century Mobile Architecture*, an inventory by the Mobile City Planning Commission; *Lessons from the Big House*, by Frye Gaillard; and *Remember Mobile*, by Caldwell Delaney and C.S. Whistler.

Among the helpful periodicals and brochures were the following: *The Magazine Antiques*, September 1977; *Old Mobile*; *The Mobile Bay Monthly*; *Looking South*; *The Journal of Negro History*, October 1927; and the Mobile Chamber of Commerce Statistical Abstract.

Special thanks also to the following individuals: Pinky Bass, Nedra Stimpson, Ann Adams, Marion Adams III, Bert Milling Jr., and Helen Amante Gaillard. Thanks also to John and Amy Rogers whose book on Charlotte served as a model, and to Amy Rogers for making the introduction to Arcadia.